Whispers

of the

Wind

Book and cover design by CE Design · New York
Cover illustration by Victor Guillermo Malta

I.S.B.N. 1-882573-09-9
Library of Congress Catalog Card Number: 97-60584

Printed in the United States

Victor Guillermo Malta

Whispers of the Wind

ZINNIA BOOKS

1997

DEDICATION

I wish to dedicate this book
to the souls of those people,
scattered all over the world,
who have died
during the pursuit of freedom.

Since freedom is still a rare commodity
for those rated as second class citizens of the world,
my book is dedicated
to them—the sufferers in a society
where tolerance and kindness are something alien.

- Victor Guillermo Malta
New York
August 29, 1996

FOREWORD

Long ago while reading an old encyclopedia, I stumbled across a section on the history of slavery and the slave trade. This topic has engulfed the world in intense emotion within the last two centuries, and no words can ever really convey the true suffering of those men and women who have lived in the misery of captivity.

There is a great deal of material available to the serious student that has been written by scholars, who have devoted their lifetimes to the study of slavery throughout the world. What I have written in the following pages offers no special analysis nor justifications for the crimes of history. My purpose here is solely to engage the mind of the reader—to present a collection of dramatized situations that reveal some of the important issues pertaining to slavery and its trade.

Victor Guillermo Malta

1

Here is home,

Just a place to dwell,

To dream,

To enjoy,

Whether a house,

A hut,

A tent,

On top of a hill,

A jungle,

Or a town;

Family and things

To linger in our minds,

And forever and ever

Our home sweet home.

2

Beat all drums with a mighty strength,
Mind not the sounds,
Thunder will carry their clamor.

The elders, the women, and the children,
Intone chants to invoke God's mercy;
It is the same,
The slavers relentlessly are walking the land.
No time to escape.
Ruthless forces will be destiny forever,
Of a mute, blind, and alien world.

3

Trembling,

Wishing to stop beneath the trees.

To sing songs of despair.

To rest.

To wet the lips by the winding shores

Of a river.

But the trees are scrambled with the wind,

And the rivers are hidden in the mist.

4

Walk, walk, and walk;

Look up, look down, but keep walking.

No excuse to die,

Keep walking.

Walk beyond the lust of Mother Nature,

Further from the twilights of all landscapes,

Wander for centuries on the roads of the world.

Chains that are twisted around the heart

Will keep on clinking,

Clinking,

Clinking,

Clinking.

5

Path of blisters

Left behind times.

The sea,

The moaning sea,

From which the precious seed of life is harvested;

Green waves ripples back and forth.

Its foam blends into small hills of alabaster,

Has become deaf to the rattles of the chains.

Beyond the horizon

The sun blushes with reddish color.

Souls, keep on walking,

Wrap your silence.

The chains will keep rattling on and on.

6

Slave ships nesting

On top of the green waves,

Bound for ports that are blended with left-overs

From hunger and disease.

Nefarious accomplices!

Men, women, children will be sold,

For gold,

Silver,

For wine.

Sharp-tongued auctioneers will scream

In the afternoon,

Fair price!

Madness attached over the sun

Has selected one more sin

To be pasted onto the pages of History

7

Voices shouting.

Whips are singing songs of ridges

on the bodies,

Hiss, and stop,

Hiss, and hit again.

The men,

Women,

The children,

Cannot cope against the anger of the whips.

Souls are bleeding,

Stop,

Stop,

Stop;

The trail left behind is full of bodies.

The whips hiss and hit again with more anger.

8

Wide,
The entrails of those barbarian ships.

Inside,
Death howls in the dark.

Outside,
The mocking laugh of men
Speaking with a tongue full of riddles.

Among the few slaves that are still alive,
The thoughts of freedom become something alien.

Strange how the faces of their friends, children, and elders,
Touch their minds;
It is a flick in time that lingers in the darkness
Till no more tears come out from the eyes.

9

Shoved

Among another aliens,

Language is unstitched from life.

Whispers,

Shapeless sounds,

Silence,

Screams:

Enemies!

Enemies full of malice

That worship only lust, gold, silver, and wine;

This is a savage game,

To crush a human

Then to sell him at the best price.

10

Wretched rats that infest the belly of the barbarian ship;
An awful presence
That knit screams of the walking shadows.
Unseen tears from someone's eyes.

Silence starts to break.
A casual conversation,
Strength to curse the agony.

The rats hungry crawl back and forth over the bodies.
Their sharper teeth furiously feast
on the flesh of corpses.

Claws of doom seem to linger in the air.
Yet life with its strength keeps watch over the hours.

11

On deck
The rain stretches the sails.

The skipper and his crew sing songs of joy.
Inside the cabin they start to play love
With few of the females.

Only one though.

A voice is raised in the night.
Why do you take so long?
My watch is coming soon,
I want to have it now.

In vain the women try to fight
Or to endure all the restless eyes,
Hands,
Smells,
The sadistic ritual that goes on and on, and on,
Will go forever on those nights.

The ship keeps on dancing over the tip of darkness.

12

Indifference,
Corpses covered with hours.

Shadows bent,
Extent of chains;
Abandon floods reality.
Ambiguity lifts time.

Faces like white pain smear the shadows;
Look up
Above imagination,
Scream,
Talk to God,
Ask for justice.

Selected to be punished for crimes that do not exist;
Condemned to walk the shores of the scorn.

Damned!
Damned!
Damned!

13

Where is home?

A place where the heart is nursed with love,

Mothers,

Sisters,

Fathers,

Friends.

Home gift of God where time is absent;

Whether a hut bathed with sounds of drums,

A hill blazing with green lust,

Mountains with birds,

To chase the sun, the winds, the night,

Or walk the beaches.

To give love.

Home where life is a cycle

For good,

For bad,

Where smiles fill the walls.

Home,

Home,

Sweet home.

14

Sin,
Is to be somewhat a little different.

Look into the fairness of judgments,
Do not distrust innocence.

Grief is folded among tears,
It teaches the bitter soul to implore for clemency.

The night with silence always grow darker.

Up on deck the crew howls at the moon,
They are full of rum screaming wrong for right.

15

Life!

Mistress of one day

It lasts one spark, one thunder.

Think,

It gives so little for which the pay is dear.

Another day is now for which the name is changed,

Conspicuously call it

Hope,

Hours keep on sliding over the darkness,

Leaving behind stress.

It is a carcass that fills the thoughts;

No doubt that yesteryear was better than tomorrow.

BOOK TWO

16

We'll never have what we claim

We own,

Because,

It is in our hands just like a loan.

17

Faces,

Eyes that show anxiety in their lines,

Winds that carry

another notch in time.

Beyond,

A red half sun that promises freedom.

This time

No chains to rattle,

Only reminiscences,

Rolling green hills patched with homes,

The walks of yesteryears.

The friends,

Family,

Pubs,

The streets with cobblestones,

Bits of the past exchanged for new life.

18

Greet all the newcomers,

One by one.

Smile,

Say: Hello.

Tell them:

"It is of the utmost importance

For you people,

To understand that you have reached a new land,

A new continent.

You will have a chance

To speak about your issues.

You are strong,

You can make something precious of this land."

Sorry! No one comes around this park.

The night is here,

No moon, no stars, no lights,

It is so cold in fact,

A new country.

19

Distrust,

Terseness,

Distorted far away smiles,

Screams,

"I want those children for my farm."

"I will pay a fair price."

Voices thundering an offer,

In a short time all the children of the newcomers

Are sold.

Cry!

Misery of Destiny,

Brothers and sisters shifted among patches of a world

Sold to be mistresses,

Servants in a house,

To die a thousand times from sunrise to sundown.

Sold willingly by fathers, and mothers,

An alien land where by habit it will be called home.

20

Walk at ease,

Sons and daughters of misery,

Leave behind the sorrows

Show only virtues;

Be swift like the winds or the whip will kiss your shoulders;

Life will wrap you around if you listen,

Or death will embrace you with its quietness.

New masters will give you love,

Will share with you,

Their food,

Their hopes.

Sing songs of joy now that life start to bloom.

21

Dreams,

Ephemeral fantasy

Entombed

Among scars,

Patches of lust dancing in the soul,

To torment,

To judge,

To mock with thoughts of hidden faces.

Tired,

Shouting despair,

Dispossessed from the growth of civilization,

Lingering around menial things,

Rewarded with scraps,

Turned away from the corners of hope,

Still, dreams with loud voice.

Listen.

22

Ask,

What is a real name?

Strange sounds,

Letters embracing speech to give the sensation of existence.

A name picked at random from the Bible;

Slapped in the face,

Attached to the neck?

Indeed, strange sounds.

The soft name of the mother

Pronounced like a breeze that stirs the tall grass

At the edge of a river;

The names of brothers and sisters

Which sound like thunder

When the father,

Calls them on the side of the mountain.

The mind grows dim with pain

Trying to remember a new name

That avoids meaning in the language.

23

Work,

Work,

Work,

Summer bursting with bright sun,

Hot winds,

The fields are pregnant.

Streams of green aisles full of cotton,

Milk to be sucked from the breast of Mother Earth,

Dust.

Pain,

Work until the sun is absent,

Intone hymns of sweat,

Mother Earth,

Embrace the dreams of men!

24

Lonely,

Simple at heart,

Branded by the times.

So close to earth,

Greedy for her love.

Embrace her,

Touch her mountains,

They are gigantic breasts,

Be engulfed in the juices of her lakes,

Love her,

Her trees, her birds,

Her oceans,

Caves, gorges, forests,

Then die a peaceful death.

25

To travel the cycles of life,
Like the wind.

Earth,
Beloved earth,
Open the doors,
Chant songs of love,
Speak
With all the words, and signs that have been forgotten.

To dance around your waist,
To jump full of joy,
To watch the brooks,
To caress the trees and drink the honey.
To forget the chains that tighten the thoughts,
Finally,
To be rescued from the claws of time.

26

Crucial assumption.

How to explain the unreasonable

Which preys upon the reason?

To talk,

To share thoughts of purpose,

To identify despair,

To share sympathy beyond imagination.

Crouched

Wearing rags,

Weak from work from dawn to dusk.

To travel roads of loneliness,

In the pursuit of sterile demands.

Outsider!

People post anonymity over that presence.

27

Patience.

The world has become frantic with sounds of thoughts.

Thunder

Fill the air.

Beats of hearts dance inside the hours,

Wind blows clamor beyond pages of history.

Who carried the three thousand pound stones

To build the pyramids?

Slaves!

Across the desert;

Slaves!

Millions of stones,

Slaves! Slaves! Slaves!

Chirping sounds that disturb lightly the serenity of earth.

Thoughts wrapped with dry blood of ancestors.

Beautiful must it have been

For them to think about freedom.

28

Distant echoes,

Wrinkles on the face of the Earth.

Duty to love the world.

Drunken paths of the Andes,

Wind, sun, dust,

Voices speaking with forgotten sounds,

Invisible presence,

Andean Indians,

Imperfect crew,

Remnants of an empire that walks, and walks,

Wearing the colors of rainbows.

29

Innocence.
Part time freedom
Full schedule slave.
With ideas of a worker
With nonexisting wages.

He walks among the sheep that do not belong to him.
Inca from another time.
Wakes up early
Knowing that nobody will realize that he existed;
Walks with music tangled in the beats of his heart,
Tyranny has been telling him false stories of understanding,
The sensuous joy of life is just a jest in his strife.

BOOK THREE

30

To hate

Will mock the senses;

It clings, and clings in dreams, and blooms in thorns,

Then,

Pain is real, and it overruns love.

31

When the sun strikes the body,

It glitters in all its sweetness,

Hair shines with the splash of moonlight.

Light skin,

Smiles to legitimate despair,

Blue eyes wrinkle with the touch of the hours,

Black hearts deteriorate with disappointments every second.

In reality,

Everyone holds in their hands a fraction of a world;

An alien world,

Where the duty is to preclude happiness,

In order to give the chills of discrimination.

Misery!

32

To be a free man

Is to wear in life the proud colors of a banner;

To share

The imaginations with the world.

To walk on the shores,

Stumbling over dreams

With no pain,

No hate.

Grief is only a word,

A whisper of the wind.

As a free man,

Think,

To be a slave is only a prank

Played by gods with narrow minds.

33

It is true that hearts have been mislead,

The chill still there.

Thorns embedded

Into minds and souls of angry people.

The echo of those voices

Incite the imagination of a world

Where evidently

Just to think,

Is wrong.

Eventually,

The only response to that cry

Will be,

Despair of the winds.

34

Walk happy under the sun,

All windows are bathed with splendor;

Walk among people

Without feeling the spectral horror

Of being watched.

Face the sun,

With no wrath against the world;

People smile most of the time,

Even when their hearts are bleeding

With an empty hope of reasoning.

35

To watch,

The vain role of men,

Whispering to the winds the ambiguity of their dreams.

To miss the greener grass,

Stalks of corn,

The cotton aisles,

Mills with their strong smell of rum,

Melody of drums with chants of youth at night,

Women with strong backs

Laying down on the grass next to the trees,

Naked,

With breasts like obsidian,

Like alabaster,

With hips shining with the light of the moon,

Ready for the furtive and frenzied lovemaking.

36

Anguish!

To wander throughout the years

From north to south,

From east to west.

Not to look, to feel, to enjoy

Just like a beggar;

Singing songs of trust with the music of the cannons;

To stand aloof wrapped in pain,

Talking to the wind about love and freedom.

To sleep,

If it is possible to sleep long enough,

It might destroy the sarcasm that surrounds existence.

37

To sleep,
To dream of odd and twisted shapes.

Night after night to go and walk
The empty streets of the world.
Streets full of people that walk with blind obedience
Within limits of pretentious emotions.
A changed world,
A whimsical world
Where no possible solutions were allowed.
To think of a fragmented death every second,
Futility of trying to give love,
A love that will last forever.
Tomorrow,
Is only a mushroom cloud away,
Nobody will have time to harvest sorrows,
Neither will the chosen ones have time to love
Before they'll vanish.

38

Acid rain is falling,

The rain is here,

There,

Everywhere.

The rain covers the streets,

The forest,

The birds lay dead among the leaves,

Inside empty stores,

Among cans full of food.

Acid rain hits the face,

The eyes,

The whole body is wet with blood;

Wet sand starts to drip from the corner of the eyes,

The sand is black,

Black algae cover the hair,

The blisters cover every wrinkle of the body.

The hands have become so sticky

From pulling dead dreams out of the imagination.

39

In the middle of the dream, scream,
Scream!
Give some love at the same time.
Do not make war;
War is not civilized.

Look around,
People crowding in the name of different religions,
Hating,
Cursing each other's gods
Preaching the morality they lack.

In another corner of the dream:
Soldiers—desperadoes—try to die in a name of a banner,
While men standing on top of imaginary platforms
Are screaming the high ideals of their political party.

Meanwhile, famished children are opening with their teeth
Cans of contaminated food.
There is no time to give love,
No time at all, no time, the time is vanishing slowly.

40

To wake up,

Then, to be engulfed in another dream.

A crazy dream,

A clumsy dream,

A dream which is full of evil creatures.

That have taken possession of everyone's hopes.

They were walking like figures all stretched out

With smiles over their faces,

Looking with a hateful glance at their wristwatches,

With their hands holding guns.

Their faces so young and old.

There in the dream they stood silently,

Watching each other's faces,

Forcing the men of the world

To wear a uniform

Which had the strangest, greenish color.

41

In the dream

The evil creatures are striking a raging world.

They buckled with complicity

Everyone.

To notice the obsessive endeavor that engulfs everybody.

Just to obtain personal rewards,

It is a horrible shriek that teases the mind.

After these reflections

Without enjoying the spectacle,

Sit in the middle of the dream

Watch the world that has started to shrivel.

42

It was not a dream!

All splendors of life
Fade away among the clouds of war.
Then share togetherness
With those that have been despised.

Destiny so strange!

To strive for survival indeed,
A common chance for all.

No time for thoughts,
It is the afternoon of the desires.
No next day.
Invoke the creator of all things
To help,
To understand,
The priviledge to kill someone
To be decorated,
To be called a friend by the comrades.

43

The sun rises soft every morning,

The winds have become defiant,

The clouds show their faces smeared up

With some forgotten war paint.

Behold Mother Earth!

It seems that your land has become smaller;

Your marshes,

Rivers,

Mountains,

Valleys,

All are filled with thunder and lightning of the cannons.

Behold Mother Earth!

All the nations of the world are tortured with pain.

In vain they all show pride with their banners;

The end of the road is death.

44

The business of war,

Make a line in order to die;

No questions,

Obey.

Obey.

Obey.

March,

Fight against the enemy,

Kill those children.

They belong to the other side.

Old enough to kill, and be killed.

To get married,

To have children of their own.

March!

Just march.

With faces of undefined color

Eyes hard like granite,

Strike with the boots, the cobblestone streets.

Go, march,

Fix the thoughts against the neck of the front soldier.

The sweat covers the forehead.

The afternoon of life.

45

No tears,
Embrace them,
Perhaps,
It is the last time.

Let them make love,
Let them enjoy life now,
Death may want to kiss them "Goodnight".

They love life,
Illusory thoughts;
The hours are sliding from their dreams to fast.

No time to bid them farewell;
Embrace them like ivy to stones,
Enjoy what is left till dawn comes.

46

Carry-on,

Carry-on men from all races, and all colors.

Hold hands with everyone,

Be able to make unreasonable choices.

War!

Everyone detach the sentiments

Be concerned with the issues at hand;

Show strength,

The world has to recognize a great power.

Bless the war,

The war carries the present.

Love death as a companion,

Above,

God will just watch, and watch, and watch.

47

To hear at all hours
The thunder of the cannons.
Bullets whistling by the ears.

To gaze at death sprawled among companions
Silken hands carrying the stench of rotten corpses.

To be beyond the threshold of all reflections.
Just to dump dreams.

Bless the war,
Only one race,
One color, and one language.
Just one name,
The human race that has become so tired;
Existence is on hold,

Beyond, above,
Absurd,
Only war planes competing with the stars.

48

Death,
No mercy at all,
With leisure it walks the twisted channels
Where humans hide from other humans.

Bodies with no eyes
Looking into the emptiness of the firmament,
Some with no entrails,
Mud only,
With flies feasting fiercely on the carrion.

Death has brought temporary equality
Within the human race,
No sides to choose,
No time to think.

To wake up in the morning
Smiling,
After a few hours, either to be mentioned as a casualty
Or, to glance at the stiff bodies of comrades.

49

Dead men were wrapped with wool blankets,
The last and most precious
Possession that was obtained.

Morning glare covers the silver caskets,
They are laid down in rows
Next to each other.
Their human faces have the paleness of death;
Pictures in an old album that have started to fade away.

To know all of them,
Just people that have been dispossessed
Of the rights to enjoy life.
Dreams of wives, children,
A job, a home,
Shattered.

The lines were long.
To think in those moments
Of those long lines to buy tickets
For a baseball game.

50

Time is here,

When cash, checks, and plastic

Won't buy dreams.

Postcards from home are wrinkled,

Stained,

They will be disposed of with the garbage.

The letters from wives,

Girlfriends,

Will have to be returned, stamped, "Sorry not available."

No flowers.

Touch of cold only, that stiff life.

Now the party starts for the pallbearers,

The grave diggers are dancing with their shovels

In no time the show will be over.

BOOK FOUR

51

Homecoming,

Sweet grapes,

To share the rainbow.

52

Ribbons, and medals;

Confetti, and smiles.

Detachment from death, from time, from sour dreams;

Only sweet grapes,

To enter now the lines of the triangle.

To wear a big smile with creative eyes,

Enjoy new shoes,

To walk along the light.

53

Hero!

What is the name of the war where you lost your legs?

Nobody remembers!

Where was the place that you were chosen to face

A human enemy who was burdened with the weight

Of his own dreams?

You are the only one who remembers!

Some teachers might tell the children about that war

That nobody wants to remember.

Too tired

To look at the ribbons,

To play with the medals,

To look at his legs.

Those legs left on the ground which had a strange name.

Look at him

A hero,

He came from a war.

54

Go to the park,

Sit with the reflection of the thoughts.

Linger on the homecoming

Victorious;

The younger and the older walk at the edge

Of the rainbow,

Will they listen to the ballads

That the strings of the soul are intoning?

From the corners of the windows

The children with awe look at the parade,

Stretch their hands out,

Just a speck of wind powders their lips.

55

Speak,

Spiritual values of ordinary things,

Sensitivity of the triangle.

To find that liberty is always a fashion

With the shape of workers.

Offices showing big smiles,

Big cigars contaminating

The waiting in line for an appointment.

Chairs that swivel with the way of emptiness;

The big desk commanding respect from sterile resumes,

Words that jumble among fat lips to chant,

"Maybe tommorrow."

There,

To stand, and watch those words

Carving wrinkles onto the soul.

56

To love all the brothers of the world,

Regardless of the anguish

That creeps into them every minute!

Futile duty,

Misunderstanding has crowned life with damp air.

To walk at times with the reality of a purpose;

To think that no one hears the sounds of the thoughts,

That no one tried to find possible solutions,

Life grumbles full of despair.

Sweet and sour grapes from the field,

Engendered with the sweat of the sun

Running down the eyebrows.

The time of chants has come

With the beats of happy moments.

Intone epithalamions.

Brothers of the world

Be able to share with me your sweet laughter,

Your sour sorrows.

Let's talk about our forgotten history,

We are aliens by ancestry in the land;

Let's smile;

Remember,

For sure, we'll die for our banner

When the need becomes a cause.

57

Free men,

Why keep a record of the times the thunder pounds?

The birds that died long ago

Hatched new springs.

No more dusty roads to walk hiding with the thorns,

No more morning dew

Just to wet the despair of the empty soul,

No more prayers to gods with names that the language

Has forgotten.

The sounds of sweet songs fill the churches of the world,

The children in the schools

Sing hymns praising their banners.

The wives run along the aisles of happiness,

The kitchens of the world burst with the flavor of spices.

58

Brave heart that flirts with death every hour
To waste time vainly with the past.

People and cars are going so fast.

To feel entangled in a revolving door,
Spacing life with dreams embedded in the past.
To wait for a moment when the notes of a song
Will bend the times that are getting too long?

Life is so short.
To accomplish what we hope for,
Why feel so cold,
At the edge of the curb?
The light is green.

The world yonder keeps its flames.

59

Still persisting with the struggle?

Forsake the dreams of being forlorn.
Fierce fanatics with piercing eyes
Will unravel hate against the bridges of the world,
Against the pigeons
That put droppings on their parked cars,
Gulls that brag to the solitude of the sea,
Fish that scream their right to swim,
Ladies dressed in white,
Big limousines that keep rolling on,
Big men smoking cigars,
They complain about hopes long departed,
Walk around holding hands with their dusty dreams.
Feeling as if in captivity,
In chains.
Nothing has changed; life is a mockery for them.

Beware!

60

A sea of blood ebbs, and flow;
Ripples the veins.
To be filled with anguish
Because we think we are getting old
In a world where hate is bread.

Look at the faces of modified mockery,
What can be done to ease the diffidence?
The hearts with chill are full of emptiness,
Tomorrow,
The men and women will tangle with their shadows,
They will embrace their hopes in Main Street,
They will walk, and walk, and walk,
To contemplate the stars in the celestial game,

Be at ease,
Love the asphalt,
The barking dogs, the rain,
The collectors of garbage,
You are still young.

61

Ellis Island, New York City,

San Francisco,

South of the border.

Races of men coming,

Wearing only names

Walking,

Swimming,

Round faces,

Slanted eyes,

White, green, blue, yellow, didn't matter.

They had the right to walk the towns,

To breathe, to dream, to love, to work;

Even to die.

Schools.

Children striving eagerly for the perception of a new land.

Children with rights to judge, to create

To lead a new world.

The "Promised Land."

62

The sweetness of life for some men has left
Fruitless, their dreams.

Born earnest to compete for the maturity of hopes;
Those men feel that they have been shuffled,
Left sitting on a bench,
Forgotten by posterity,
Without success,
Because some human power creeps over the land.
No rights.
That this perverse stand of moral conscience
Is the weapon used against them
Erasing in this fashion the hope for which to strive.

Children of the children,
Wake up.
The younger generations will have to play the game.
By destiny we all are slaves of something precious,
Of something evil.
Feel tired and old
Having wasted precious time wearing voided traditions.

63

I walk the streets smiling at everyone.

I look at people trying to find some kind of difference;

What do I see?

Round faces, skinny faces, flat faces;

Wearing blue eyes, green eyes, brown eyes,

Long noses, short noses,

Fat bodies,

Small and skinny bodies, with fat or skinny legs;

Men, women, children, old people;

Just people,

They walk looking at the sky,

Powdering their eyes with bright lights,

Wearing smart or meek airs.

It seems that they have abandoned their thoughts

At the mouth of the times.

Those people are a collection of life

That is vanishing slowly, just like me.

I keep on smiling when I look at their faces

Bathed with the early morning.

64

Chant for peace,

With all the brothers, sisters, children of the world,

With the young,

The old,

With the children of their children.

Sweetness in the promiscuity of the hearts,

To journey over paths of uninterrupted dreams;

The wind carrying the chants beyond the world;

The sun burning the faces,

The sweat bathing the bodies,

Endurance as a feeling of the heart;

Chant in unison,

Pluralize the heartbeats all over the earth.

One chant for peace, forever peace.

Peace.

Peace.

Peace!

65

I wish I could go to sleep for a few centuries,
Then, if I am able to wake up,
I might be able to sing:
Children,
Listen to my voice,
I am bringing peace for you.

My voice is the wind that travels inside your soul,
Inside your hearts,
Your minds.
I intone melodies of peace.

I will cherish your life with dreams of love;
No more suffering, no more anguish.
I will cast with the fire of my notes
The kind of songs embedded in your hopes.

You, that walk the cities, towns, deserts of the world,
You, that travel by air over the seas
Or dwell on mountains,
Peace, only peace.
Children, listen to the melody of my poetry.

.